ISBN 978-1-334-22440-9
PIBN 10314108

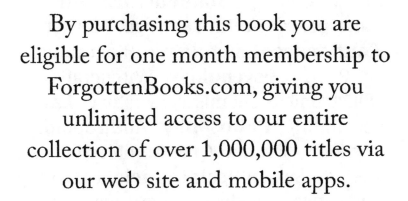

This book is DUE on the last date stamped below

PROPOSED CHANGES

IN THE

METHODS OF TEACHING ARITHMETIC

IN THE COMMON SCHOOLS

19206

FRANK H. HALL

AUTHOR OF THE WERNER ARITHMETICS, THE HALL ARITHMETICS
THE ARITHMETIC READERS, ETC.

WERNER SCHOOL BOOK COMPANY

EDUCATIONAL PUBLISHERS

NEW YORK   CHICAGO   BOSTON

FROM THE REPORT

. OF THE

COMMITTEE OF TEN

"The Conference [on Mathematics] consisted of one government official and university professor, five professors of mathematics in as many colleges, one principal of a high school, two teachers of mathematics in endowed schools, and one proprietor of a private school for boys. The professional experience of these gentlemen and their several fields of work were various, and they came from widely separated parts of the country; yet they were unanimously of opinion that a *radical change in the teaching of arithmetic* was necessary."

ARITHMETIC: HOW TO TEACH IT.

Whence Comes the Demand for a Change in the Methods of Instruction?

The "Committee of Ten" was appointed at the meeting of the National Educational Association in Saratoga in July, 1892. Its chairman was Charles W. Eliot, President of Harvard University. Dr. William T. Harris, Commissioner of Education, was a prominent member of the committee. *Committee of Ten.*

The "Conference on Mathematics" appointed by this committee "consisted of one government official and university professor, five professors of mathematics in as many colleges, one principal of a high school, two teachers of mathematics in endowed schools, and one proprietor of a private school for boys. *Conference on Mathematics.* The professional experiences of these gentlemen and their several fields of work were various, and they came from widely separated parts of the country; yet they were unanimously of opinion that a *radical change in the teaching of arithmetic* was necessary." The members of this conference simply formulated and voiced the common judgment on this subject—the judgment of the leaders in educational thought and of intelligent men of affairs everywhere.

McLellan and Dewey, in *The Psychology of Number*, speak of "a growing impatience with the McLellan and Dewey. meager results of the time given to arithmetic in the traditional course of the schools."

Business men very generally deplore the lack of ability on the part of youthful employees fresh from Business Men. the schools to figure accurately. Great emphasis has hitherto been given to the commercial side of arithmetic, and yet pupils are inefficient, a majority of them at least, to a remarkable degree, in the figure manipulation required in ordinary business. Said a prominent Bostonian: "All children are taught to cipher; yet in my selection of office boys I find that very few know how to apply the art of ciphering to the work of life."

High-school teachers are wont to complain of the inefficiency of the mathematical training received by High-School Teachers. their pupils while in the grades. They find large numbers of these pupils, possibly a majority, deficient (1) in ability to discern quantitative relation, and (2) in skill in accurate ciphering. They demand improvement in these two respects.

This demand, then, for a *radical change* in the method and curriculum, so far as arithmetic is concerned, is of no narrow origin. It is as extensive as the educational world itself, and as intensive as the combined expression of the mathematician, the psychologist, the representative business man, and the high-school teacher can make it.

What Changes in Matter are Desirable?

The first recommendation made by the Conference on Mathematics, appointed by the Committee of Ten, is, that "the course in arithmetic be **Abridgment** at the same time abridged and enriched: **Necessary.** abridged by omitting entirely those subjects which perplex and exhaust the pupil without affording any really valuable mental discipline; and enriched by a greater number of exercises in simple calculation and in the solution of concrete problems."

This Conference suggested the curtailment or entire omission of compound proportion, cube root, obsolete denominate quantities, duodecimals, and the **What** greater part of commercial arithmetic. It **Omitted.** further suggested that in such subjects as profit and loss, bank discount, and simple and compound interest, examples not easily made intelligible to the pupil should be omitted. In these recommendations the Conference has voiced the sentiment of thoughtful teachers everywhere.

Pupils in the grammar grades have been required to memorize definitions, when, because of the immaturity of their minds, they were unable to see through the definitions the things defined. They have been required to solve problems of whose uses and applications they had no clear conception. Again and again they have lost sight of what they were trying to do in trying to find out how to do it. The mere manipulation of figures has been allowed to absorb their attention and to exhaust their energies.

In many instances pupils have been well taught in the primary grades and in the so-called "mental arithmetic" work. They have learned in a small

Too Much Mere Figure Work. way to see magnitude relation and to express it in number. But no sooner are they admitted to the class in "written arithmetic" than they are confronted with long rows of figures— to them mere figures — and with these they are expected to juggle, and to obtain other figures called "the answer."

Says General Francis A. Walker: "Who of us has not seen in the hands of children eleven, twelve, and

Work Too Difficult. thirteen years of age examples in compound and complex fractions which were more difficult than any operation which any bank cashier in the city of Boston has occasion to perform in the course of his business from January to December? The most jagged fractions, such as would hardly ever be found in actual business operation—e. g., $\frac{11}{29}$ or $\frac{13}{37}$—are piled one on top of another to produce an unreal and impossible difficulty; and the child, having been furnished with such an arithmetical monstrosity, is set to dividing it by another compound and complex fraction as unreal and ridiculous as itself. All this sort of thing in the teaching of young children is either useless or mischievous. It is bad psychology, bad physiology, and bad pedagogics."

The leading educators of the state of Wisconsin

Views of Wisconsin Educators. recently recommended, among other things, the following in relation to the course of study in arithmetic;

Work in fractions below the fifth grade mainly oral.

No long division below fifth grade with divisors of more than two figures.

Omit greatest common divisor entirely as separate topic.

Omit longitude and time. Teach the principles of this in connection with geography

Omit reduction, addition, subtraction, multiplication, and division of denominate numbers as separate topics.

Limit taxes, insurance, and duties to simplest cases and explanation of terms.

Give very little attention to problems in interest.

Omit true discount, and take only the first case in bank discount.

Omit cube root and its applications, except such as can be done by inspection.

From the foregoing it will be apparent that the current of thought sets strongly in favor of the elimination of much that has heretofore been regarded as essential. "For ten years," says Superintendent J. M. Greenwood, "the process of elimination has been going on, and we have not seen the end of it yet."

Unmerited Criticism to be Expected by Those Who Adopt These Recommendations.

There will necessarily be some embarrassment for those who accept and adopt such abridgment as is herein recommended. There are examiners and examiners. Many of these learned their elementary mathematics before this process of elimination began, and have not yet come into line with those educators who favor abridgment. These will persist in confronting the pupils with problems that belong to the parts eliminated. The mechanically taught pupil may

be able to reduce a three-story combination of compound and complex fractions to a simple fraction in
less time than it can be done by the thoughtful pupil.
He may "get answers" to problems in compound
proportion and cube root and its applications (if the
problems are in every way regular and fall under
some rule that has been memorized) more readily than
the pupil who has learned to see magnitude and magnitude relation in his figures—who thinks.   Hence
improved methods and pupils taught in accordance
with them are liable to unmerited criticism from those
whose standard is radically different from that presented by the Conference on Mathematics appointed
by the Committee of Ten.

What Enrichment is Desirable?

The work must be enriched as well as abridged—
"enriched by a greater number of exercises in simple
calculation and in the solution of concrete
problems." The pupil must be exercised
in seeing quantitative relation.   The emphasis must be put upon this phase of the work rather
than upon mere figuring.   The figure processes must
be learned, and the pupil must be taught to compute
with absolute accuracy.   But from the first he must
learn to regard figure manipulation as a convenience
in discerning exact relation.   He figures
not that he may learn to cipher, but that
he may compare quickly and accurately the
various magnitudes in which he is interested—magnitudes of time, of space, of intensity, of weight, of

More Concrete Work.

Ciphering to be Made Less Prominent.

value.   Take away the figures, and there yet remains
mathematics — arithmetic — number.   Ciphering will
not be discarded (though it would be possible to complete the real work in arithmetic without it), but it
must be relegated to its proper place in mind development.   It must be treated as a convenience in obtaining mathematical results.

The arithmetical instruction in the grades must be
enriched, just as the teaching of reading has already
been enriched, by leading the pupils to see through
the symbols to that for which the symbols stand; by
using the symbols to express thought.   Thought is
the main thing in mathematics as well as in *Magnitude*
reading.   In either of these branches of *Relation More*
study one may play with symbols or work *Prominent.*
with symbols, and not think.   "Thinking is discerning
relation."   In mathematics the things related are
magnitudes.   Leave these out — juggle with mere
figures—and the subject is impoverished; put them
in, and the subject is enriched.

Number Symbols and Their Content.

The symbols of number employed in arithmetic are
words, as *one, two, seven, twenty-four*, etc.; and
figures, as 1, 2, 7, 24, etc.   While it is true that these
symbols stand for number and that number expresses
ratio, it is also true that they may suggest *Double*
magnitude.   They may properly stand in *Significance*
of Number
thought for measured magnitudes.   For *Symbols.*
instance, the number six (or the figure 6) may call
into consciousness a magnitude that is six times

some unit of measurement, or it may suggest the relation (ratio) of that magnitude to its unit of measurement.   The following from *The Common Sense of the
Exact Sciences** will help to make this plain:

> The formulæ of arithmetic and algebra are capable of
> double interpretation.   For instance, such a symbol as 3
> meant, in the first place, a number of letters, or men, or
> any other thing; but afterwards was regarded as mean-
> ing an operation; namely, that of trebling anything.
> And so the symbol $\frac{15}{12}$ may be taken either as meaning so
> much of a foot, or as meaning the operation by which a
> foot is changed into fifteen inches.

These symbols, then, have a double significance—
a possible double content.   Sometimes they should
carry with them the thought of magnitude; sometimes the thought of ratio.   Too often they carry
nothing.   They are empty.

In the varying content of these number symbols
there is an element of pedagogical danger.   To the
Element   teacher they may mean the one thing; to
of Danger.   the pupil the other, or possibly nothing.
He figures, but he does not see relation.   He ciphers,
but he does not think.   How can he think—discern
relation—when the symbols which he employs are
empty?   How can he compare when the terms of the
comparison are not in consciousness—only the symbols of the terms?

It is often said that we think in symbols.   So we
do; but they are symbols of something, and unless we
are able to think into them that for which they stand,
our thinking is not of the highest order.   To make

*W. K. Clifford—D. Appleton & Company.

our thinking of value, we must be able to interpret the symbols employed.

When Should the Number Symbols Suggest Magnitude and when Suggest Ratio?

On page 76 of *The Psychology of Number,** by McLellan and Dewey, is found the following:

Psychologically speaking, can the multiplicand ever be a pure number? If the foregoing account of the nature of number is correct, the multiplicand, however written, must always be understood to express measured quantity; it is always concrete.

But if multiplicands are always concrete, so are products and addends and sums and minuends and subtrahends and differences and remainders **Pure or** and dividends. Multipliers stand for rela- **Concrete?** tion, or as Clifford puts it, for an operation. If a particular divisor is concrete, the corresponding quotient shows relation. If a particular divisor shows relation, the corresponding quotient is concrete.

The subject of arithmetic will be marvelously enriched when the number symbols bring into the consciousness of the pupil their true and appropriate content.

The Imaging of Magnitude.

The magnitude content of a number symbol at first will be a memory image — a reproduction of that which at some former time appeared in con- **Memory** sciousness through the action of the senses. **Images.** It will be an image of some cube or square or line or circle, that was presented to the senses at some par-

*D. Appleton & Company.

ticular time and in some particular place. The time and the place will at first be recalled as well as the object.

Reproducing this image again and again, using it in thinking—in comparing—at length the time element and the place element fade out, and it can be made to stand forth in consciousness as a cube, a square, a line, or a circle, without any reference to any particular

Idealized Images. sense magnitude. Such idealized images make up a stock of "mind stuff" with which the successful pupil builds new magnitudes in endless variety. The repeated reproduction of memory images of magnitude, and of the idealized images to which these, under proper instruction, soon give place, is the *sine qua non* to a proper beginning of number teaching.

But again: one may think quantity without thinking any particular *form* of magnitude. We can

Formless Images of Quantity. think $\frac{1}{2}$ as a magnitude without stopping to determine whether it is the half of a cube, a square, a line, or a circle. We may thus, without being tied down to the *forms* of sense, discriminate sharply between the one-half whose practical content is magnitude and the one-half whose content is relation. We can thus put content into number symbols, even though our images of magnitude are without definite shape. We can even think—see magnitude relation clearly — when the things related are to us literally "without form and void." So we learn to deal with abstract magnitude—abstract quantity.

Yet again: one can think two number symbols of dissimilar content, and a suggested operation, without stopping to think which of the number symbols has a magnitude content and which a ratio content. The equation, $\frac{1}{2} \times \frac{1}{4} = \frac{1}{8}$, is true, whether the $\frac{1}{2}$ or the $\frac{1}{4}$ is regarded as a symbol of magnitude. It is not necessary in practice that one should think which of these stands for magnitude and which stands for ratio; but it is necessary that *in mind training* the teacher should provide that the pupil shall not as a rule use symbols and processes which he, the learner, the one who is being trained, is unable to interpret. "We may always depend upon it," says W. K. Clifford, "that algebra which cannot be translated into good English and sound common sense is bad algebra." So arithmetic whose expressions and processes cannot be translated by the learner himself into magnitudes and magnitude relation is bad arithmetic—bad pedagogy.

Operations with Symbols.

Ability to Translate Necessary.

Number and Measurement.

The number idea has its origin in measurement. In *The Psychology of Number* * (McLellan and Dewey), page 44, the authors speak of "the process of measuring from which number has its genesis."

The teaching of number begins in measurement. The very best teachers in our primary grades now accept this as a fundamental truth, and base their practice upon it.

*D. Appleton & Company.

The uses of number end in measurement.   This is in accord with our daily experience and observation.   We learn arithmetic that we may measure—measure our wealth; measure the land and its products; measure the heights of mountains and the depths of the sea; measure heat, light, and the electric current.

Hence, in the beginning, arithmetic deals with magnitudes—something to measure.   In the end it deals with magnitudes—something to be measured.   But in the middle there has been in the past a great

Learning Figure Processes. gulf of figures and figure processes.   Many a pupil has been *figuratively* shipwrecked in crossing this gulf.   The small minority of mentally strong pupils make the passage without serious disaster.   It is just possible that the very few, the exceptionally strong ones, are even made stronger by the difficulties which they encounter.   These are the mathematicians.   They will learn mathematics, whatever may be the method of presentation.   But to the great majority it is an unfortunate experience from which they never fully recover.   The new methods demand the bridging of this gulf between the magnitude measurements in which the number idea originates and the magnitude measurements to which the arithmetical processes are to be applied; or better, perhaps, the discovery of the magnitude islands that mark *a* passage (possibly a little circuitous) across the gulf.   We have no right to allow the youthful mariner to lose sight of land for any considerable time while making this trip.

The figure processes he must learn; but to require him, to allow him, to abandon thought of magnitude while he learns to figure has its parallel in **Must not** the study of the words of a sentence with- **Abandon** **Thought of** out any attention to the thought expressed. **Magnitude.** Thought is the main thing in arithmetic as well as in language. Figures are at once the symbols of the real subjects of thought and of the relations of these subjects. To allow the pupil to juggle with these symbols for weeks and months while magnitude is either altogether omitted or thrust far into the background is fatal to good training. To teach a child long division and long multiplication and long fraction manipulation before he is made to feel the need of these processes in making measurements and in seeing magnitude relations, is not simply a waste of time: it is unpedagogical, and in many instances at least, seriously disastrous as an attempted step in mental development.

A Greater Degree of Accuracy in the Figure Processes Demanded.

The Conference on Mathematics appointed by the Committee of Ten summed up the suggestions made in their special report on arithmetic under two heads— namely, (1) *The giving of the teaching a more concrete form*, and (2) *The paying of more attention to facility and correctness in work.*

The first of these suggestions has already been considered. Taking care that the pupil associates thoughts of magnitude with figures and figure processes *is* giving the teaching "a more concrete form."

It now remains for us to consider the second sug·gestion—the securing of facility and correctness in the number processes. Heretofore the principal part of the work in "written arithmetic" has been ciphering, and yet a high degree of accuracy has not been secured. (Facility must not for a moment be considered apart from accuracy.) If we now devote less time to the mere figure processes and more time to the discerning of magnitude relation, may not the so-called improved methods result in even greater inaccuracy, and conse·quently in diminished practical efficiency?

How Secure Greater Accuracy?

The degree of approach to accuracy by a pupil does not depend so much upon the *amount* as upon the *character* of the work done. Careless facility is not merely useless: it is positively harmful. Hence, while the problems provided for the pupil may well be much more simple in respect to the amount of figuring required, the importance of accuracy must be emphasized to a very much greater degree than has

Inaccurate Work must not be Commended.
usually been the custom of teachers in the grades. Indeed, the pupil must not·be com-mended at all for inaccurate work—for work in which there is one wrong figure! It must be impressed upon him in the very beginning that cipher-ing in which there are errors has no value whatever. His task must be, not the solution of ten problems with but few errors, but rather as many problems as

he can solve without making any mistakes.   His seat work in arithmetic (and his home work, too, if any be assigned) should be, for the most part, **Kind of** mechanical, and so simple that he can con- **Seat Work** centrate his whole energy upon the matter **to be Done.** of accuracy.   It should be something that he well knows how to do, the only question being, Can he do it accurately?   In this way, and in this way only, can proper emphasis be put upon the importance of absolute correctness.

Marking Arithmetic Papers.

When papers (or slates) upon which is the work of many pupils to whom the task of copying and figuring had been assigned, are presented to the teacher for examination, it is not well for her to consider too much the *number* of errors made by each pupil.   Each paper is *right* or *wrong; perfect* or *imper-* **"Perfect" or** *fect; good* or *worthless.*   Whether it con- **"ImPerfect.'** tains one error or ten, it must be put into the im· perfect class.   All the pupils who·make mistakes in figuring must, for the moment at least, be classed together, whether the number of errors is two or ten.   In either case the work is unsatisfactory, unreliable, worthless.

In the opinion of the writer, if, in the daily tests of the ability of pupils in figuring, more than twenty-·five per cent of the papers are imperfect, the **Teacher may** teacher is at fault.   Either the lesson is too **be at Fault.** heavy, or the teacher does not sufficiently impress upon the pupils the importance of accuracy in ciphering.

The seat work, the mere practice in figuring, should be made so light, and the pupils encouraged to exer-

The Degree of Accuracy Expected. cise so much care in the doing of it, that seventy-five to ninety per cent of the papers will be perfect. When this degree of accuracy has been attained, the amount of daily work *for those pupils who usually present perfect papers,* may be somewhat increased; but in all cases and in all the grades, infallible accuracy must be the aim. At most, nothing beyond the first error should be counted to the credit of the pupil. To what length can the pupil continue to manipulate figures without one error? is the question for the examiner and for the pupil.

Old Method of Marking Papers.

Too often it has been the custom to mark a paper 90 if only one problem in ten contains an error. Often—shall I say usually?—the pupil has been taught to believe that 90 per cent of accuracy in the third grade is *good*. If only one figure was wrong, the paper was marked 95, and 95 is *excellent*. This has been the method of marking, too, in the fourth grade and in the fifth grade, and in all the grades up to and including the eighth. Then perhaps the pupil leaves school. For six years he has been taught that 95 in figure processes is *excellent;* 90, *good;* 80,

Ninety Per Cent in Accuracy is Failure. *fair*, and even 70 good enough to "pass." He goes out into the business world, to learn that 90 per cent of accuracy in figuring, instead of being *good*, is *absolute failure;* that there is no place in the world for a ninety-per-cent accountant. His inaccurate facility in the use of figures gained for him much credit in the schoolroom, but in the store it is worthless. The fact that he knows how to solve the problems, and can explain them with the "hences" and "sinces" in their proper places, is of no avail in his effort to retain his place as an accountant. He is inaccurate; hence his work is of no value whatever.

A nearer approach to accuracy may be made, not by a greater amount of careless manipulation of figures in difficult problems, but by the careful solution of many simple problems in which the principal effort on the part of both teacher and pupil is to secure results that are correct in every respect. The most important part of the work of the teacher in this effort is not the correcting of the pupil's mistakes: it is rather the training of the pupil into such careful habits that mistakes will not be made. (Many a teacher sits up at night to correct errors that she might better sit up in the daytime to prevent.)

Prevention of Errors Better than Correction.

Number Facts to be Memorized.

The primary number facts must be perfectly memorzied. (Perceive, *express*, MEMORIZE,) is the order in which the work must be done. In days gone by pupils were sometimes required to memorize and express that which they did not perceive. We must not now allow them simply to perceive and express that which they ought to memorize.

Amount to be Memorized.

The amount to be memorzied is not appalling. One new important primary number fact learned each day from the time the child enters the third grade **One Fact Each Day.** until he enters the sixth will put into his possession a stock of mathematical "memory stuff" that will compare favorably with that possessed by the average eighth-grade pupil of to-day. The imperfect memory work in many of our schools may be attributed to the facts, (1) that the advancement is not along definite lines—it is haphazard; and (2) that the work of the individual pupil is not closely enough observed and directed.

Let us make a brief survey of the field for these memory operations. There are forty-five primary **Forty-five Facts of Addition.** facts of addition. (See Werner Arithmetic. Book II., page 273).*) These facts properly memorized will carry with them the primary facts of subtraction. The boy who has perceived, expressed, and memorized the fact that 4 and 3 are 7 (′′′′ ′′′) cannot fail to know that 7 less 3 are 4, and that 7 less 4 are 3.

There are sixty-four primary facts of multiplication. (See Werner Arithmetic, Book II., note at bottom of **Sixty-four Facts of Mul-tiplication.** page 274, and tables on page 275.)† These facts properly memorized will carry with them twice sixty-four primary facts of division. The boy who has perceived, expressed, and memorized the fact that four fives equal 20 (′′′′′ ′′′′′ ′′′′′

*See Complete Arithmetic, page 443.
†See Complete Arithmetic, page 444, note 6.

$''''')$ will also know that 5 is contained in 20 four times, and that $\frac{1}{4}$ of 20 is 5.   There are, then, but one hundred nine (45+64) primary facts of number to be memorized in order that the pupil may be prepared to cipher in the fundamental processes.   At least forty-five of these (33 facts of addition and 12 of multiplication) will usually be learned by the pupil before he enters the third grade.   This leaves but sixty-four of the above to be memorized after entering the third grade— and there are nearly two hundred days in a school year!

Individual Work to be Done.

If, at the beginning of the third-grade work, the teacher would assist each pupil in taking an accurate inventory of his memory stock, and would Inventory then take care that a little is added to it to be Taken. each day, the memory side of the task mathematical would not be a formidable one.   In this work, as well as in imaging magnitude, the teacher must know as nearly as possible the exact mental status of each pupil.   She must not lose sight of the individual in the class.   She must not attempt to have her pupils memorize by platoons.

Surely, at the end of the third school year the pupil should have complete memory possession of the one hundred nine facts mentioned above.   Moreover, he should be able to use them accurately in easy examples.   *Make the ciphering work very light, and insist upon perfect accuracy*, should be the teach- The Rule. er's inflexible rule in this work and in the grade above. There should be no occasion for the criticism that "the multiplication table is neglected," and that "the pupils are interested in their work and seem very bright, but they are not accurate in the figure processes."

The Denominate Number Tables.

The pupil should be made familiar with the common units of measurement. But this cannot be accomplished by merely memorizing the words and figures of the tables. So far as possible he should use **Weights and** these units in actual measuring. Sets of **Measures.** weights and measures are even more necessary in the equipment of the schoolroom than blackboard and crayon.

Some of these units of measurement should be presented to the pupil at the very beginning of the work in arithmetic—even before its formal introduction as one of the daily subjects in the school curriculum. Many a boy excels in arithmetic because of a home **Measuring** environment by which he was early led to **for a** measure for a purpose. Perhaps he meas- **Purpose.** ured to make, or measured to sell, or measured in play. If he measured, he dealt with magnitudes, and was thus learning to consider simple, exact magnitude relations, and to express them numerically. He made the best possible beginning in arithmetic at home—in measurement.

The home surroundings of many pupils are not favorable to such foundation laying; hence the means for this must be provided at school. It is useless, it is positively harmful, to attempt the work in arithmetic without it.

The facts usually presented in the denominate number tables must not be kept from the pupil until he has learned how to "cipher in simple numbers and in fractions," and then given in doses of one or two tables a day! Such facts are an essential part of the mathematical foundation, and as such must **Measure in the Beginning.** be introduced in the beginning of the work. The pupil may be led to "measure for constructive purposes" or for destructive purposes. He may measure to buy, or measure to sell, or measure in games; but measure he must, if he is expected to discern magnitude relation and to express it numerically.

The pupil should early become familiar with the terms *inch, foot, square inch, square foot, cubic inch, cubic foot, pound, ounce, pint, quart, gallon,* **Words must Suggest Magnitudes.** etc. These terms should bring into his consciousness the magnitudes for which they stand, not necessarily the tables in which the words are found.

Reviews Necessary.

So frequently, moreover, must the pupil make use of the number facts that are usually given in the denominate number tables, and so systematically must he be led to review (see again) these facts, that **Must Become a Permanent Possession.** they will at length become to him a permanent memory possession. He may never be asked, perhaps, to commit to memory the "tables" as of yore, but the facts therein contained will be memorized before he reaches that part of the text-book in which the "tables" are usually given.

The Time to Begin the Formal Work in Arithmetic.

Since the number idea originates in measurement, and since knowledge and skill in arithmetic are acquired for purposes of measurement, it is not advisable to push to the front the mere figure processes in the early

Figures to be Kept in the Background. stages of the school work. Only as the pupil is made to feel the need of number (and figures) in discerning and expressing quantity relation should the attempt be made to enlist his interest in such exercise. True, it is possible to force the figure processes upon the attention of the pupil at a very early age, and to secure seemingly excellent results. But it is not desirable to do this. Other branches of study, if not more important, much better adapted to the needs of the young learner, should absorb the principal part of his attention in

The First Two Years of School Life. the first two years of school life. While engaged in the study of his own environment; in learning to compare, to discern relation, to think; and to express his thought in language, in drawing, in making; in learning to read and to write—he incidentally becomes familiar with such magnitudes and measurements as will make the only possible foundation for sound mathematical reasoning. Figures and figure processes should be kept in the background, and called into prominence only as their necessity is felt by the pupil in his efforts to understand his environment and to solve the child problems that naturally confront him.

When this course is pursued, and formal arithmetic

work put off until the last part of the second school year, or even to the beginning of the third, Formal Arithmetic more will be accomplished in a single term Work to be of ten or twelve weeks than would other- Deferred. wise be accomplished in twice as many months.

How to Lay the Foundation.

In the early years the arithmetical foundation may be—ought to be—laid in connection with the work in drawing, in nature study, in games, and in Drawing, construction work of all kinds.   Even if the Nature teacher is not thoughtful enough to see that Study, etc. this is done, the deferring of the .ormal arithmetic work until the beginning of the third school year will give opportunity for the child to secure much of this foundation material in the home, in the store, on the farm, in the workshop, on the playground—anywhere and everywhere that he finds something to be measured.

Hence it is to the advantage not only of the child who is being well trained in school, but of the child who is taught mechanically and unpeda- Bad Teaching gogically, that the formal work in number Worse than should not be commenced in the first years No Teaching. of school.   A little good instruction will do no harm; but bad number teaching in these years is worse by far than no teaching at all.   Too much good teaching in the discerning of quantitative relation will Too Much result inevitably in the neglect of something Good Teach- ing may be more important, and may lead the child Harmful. forever after to put too much emphasis upon the one subject of magnitude and magnitude relation.

How to Begin the Formal Number Work.

If the beginning of the regular daily work in arithmetic is deferred until the pupils are seven or eight years of age, they will have acquired incidentally many of the number facts given on pages 6 and 7 of Book I. of the Werner Arithmetics.* The teacher should **Study Each Pupil.** now "take an account of stock." She should study each pupil in respect to his imaging power and his memory acquirements.

If the pupil has been trained properly, he will be able easily to call into consciousness such magnitudes as are suggested by the following words: *inch, six inches, foot, yard, pint, quart, square, 1-inch square, 2-inch square, cube, 1-inch cube, 2-inch cube, a half-inch,* **Imaging Power.** *a half-foot, one third of a foot, two thirds of a foot, a half-hour, a quarter of an hour, a half-dollar, "a quarter," a dime, five cents, ten cents, a dozen, half a dozen,* etc. Whatever his training or his lack of training may have been, he will be familiar with some of these terms, and with many expressions of quantity and quantity relation not here given.

He will have memorized some number facts, such as 2 fives are 10, 2 twos are 4, 2 "quarters" equal **Memory of Number Facts.** a half-dollar, 15 minutes and 15 minutes are a half-hour. Perhaps he knows that 3 eggs and 3 eggs are 6 eggs, and that 6 eggs and 6 eggs are 12 eggs; that 1 half of a pie and 1 fourth of a pie are 3 fourths of a pie; that 1 half of a pie and 1 sixth of a pie are 4 sixths of a pie; that

*Substantially the same facts are given on pages 5 and 6 of Hall's Elementary Arithmetic.

a half-dollar and a "quarter" are together equal in value to 75 cents; that a 10-spot is made up of 2 fours and 2; that a 7-spot is made up of 2 threes and 1; that a half of 3 feet is 1 and 1 half feet; that 2 yards equal 6 feet; that 10 tens equal 100; that half of 100 is 50; that half of 500 is 250; that half of 5 dollars is 2 and 1 half dollars; that it takes 4 1-inch squares to make a 2-inch square, and 8 1-inch cubes to make a 2-inch cube, etc.

Werner Arithmetic, Book I., Pages 6 and 7.*

The teacher, having gained definite knowledge of the mental attainments of each pupil so far as number is concerned, should now proceed to teach **Teach New Number Facts.** such of the number facts given on pages 6 and 7 of Book I. as have not already been learned. With some pupils this will be a slight task. With others much patient effort will be required. With pupils who easily image the magnitudes considered, almost the entire strength may be concentrated upon the memory phase of the work, and the task will be speedily and well done. To pursue a seemingly similar course with pupils who do not image easily will give mere word memory results. **Mere Word Memory Results Unsatisfactory.** The number of such pupils will be relatively fewer than it would have been had the formal number work been begun in the first grade. But the teacher must at all times be on her guard lest she be deceived by the false testimony of a good memory of words and sentences.

*Hall's Elementary Arithmetic, pages 5 and 6.

Here, then, is opportunity for most important and practically valuable child-study. The teacher will

The Real Content of the Child Mind. need all the skill she can command to enable her to determine the real content of the child's mind when he says "2 thirds of 6 are 4"; "1 half of 6 is 3"; "2 quarts are 4 pints"; "3 quarts are 6 pints," etc. Many a child makes such statements almost without error in whose mind there is nothing back of the words that are uttered. The child who reads the best and who recites without hesitation may be the very one who does not really discern the relations that his words express. To recall words and sentences and repeat them glibly is one thing; to call into consciousness supposedly familiar magnitudes, to see their relation, to think and to express thought, is quite another. The first of these methods of recitation, though quite satisfactory to the teacher who does not look into the child's mind, gives responses that are mathematically and pedagogically valueless. The second calls for patient waiting, laborions imaging and comparing, and gives at first tardy responses, but with ever-increasing power.

Magnitude and Magnitude Relation to be in the Thought of the Child when Number Symbols are Employed.

The one unvarying rule in this early work is, that magnitude and magnitude relation must be in the thought of the child when he uses the number symbols. If he says, "1 half of 5 is $2\frac{1}{2}$," he must have in mind the half of 5 inches or 5 apples or 5 dollars or 5 hours—5 in the concrete. If he says, "2 thirds of

6 are 4," he must have in mind 6 objects divided into 3 equal parts, and he must see in his mental picture the 2 twos that make up the 4.   If he says, "6 is (or are) 2 thirds of 9," he must have in mind 6 objects divided into 2 equal parts, and then as many objects added to these as there are in one of the parts.

At first, of course, this work must be done with the actual objects present to the senses.   But soon, very soon, the objects must be concealed from view, and the teacher must see that their images are present in the consciousness of the child.

The Teacher and the Mere "Hearer of Recitations" Compared.

This suggests the main difference between the teacher and the "hearer of recitations."   The teacher is ever on the alert to induce imaging and the seeing of relation.   She uses objects, but **The Teacher.** she lays them aside at the earliest possible moment. She then uses the symbols for these (words and figures), and watches unceasingly for evidences of imaging power.   She discovers the pupils who are doing by word memory what they should do by seeing magnitude relation—who are trying to tell relation when the things related are not in consciousness.   These she takes back to the sense mgnitudes.   But again she quickly conceals the objects from sight, while the pupils repeat their efforts to see them with the mind's eye.   She frames her questions at first almost wholly with reference to testing and exercising the imaging power.

The "hearer of recitations," perhaps, works with objects—possibly too long—and later works with

The "Hearer of Recitations." symbols; but there is no connection between the object work and the symbol work.

The child while working with symbols images symbols, and not that for which the symbols stand. The "hearer of recitations" is satisfied if the pupil obtains *the answer*, and in explanation uses the language that is in accord with that employed by one who thinks.

The teacher "goes behind the returns." She looks into the child mind. She asks herself, "Is the

The Teacher. pupil obtaining mere figure results and reciting mere words, or is his work, his recitation, the natural expression that follows the discernment of relation—thinking?" The teacher frequently changes her own view-point, and by skillful questioning attempts to discover the real background of the child's expression. If he images and sees relation, he is encouraged to proceed. If his mental equipment is mainly word and figure pictures, she takes him back again to the things of sense.

The Primary Facts of Number must be Memorized.

The number facts given on pages 6 and 7 of Book I.* must not only be perceived by the pupil; they must be perfectly memorized. These facts, which have come to him through discernment of magnitude relation, must now be generalized, and become a permanent memory possession. He must remember that

* Elementary Arithmetic. pages 5 and 6.

7 and 5 are 12—always 12—regardless of the magnitudes to which these numbers may be applied. Such facts must now come to him by a pure act of memory, without the expenditure of any energy in imaging and combining. The symbols, $7+5$, or $\frac{7}{5}$, or $\frac{5}{7}$, must suggest 12 almost as quickly as the figures 12 suggest this number. There must be no failure in the little memory work that is necessary to the complete mastery of pages 6 and 7 of Book I. There can be no proper and advantageous committing to memory until the facts are discerned. There can be but little advancement until the facts are memorized. *Perceive*—MEMORIZE.

Werner Arithmetic, Book I., Page 9.*

Pages 6 and 7 having been mastered, the book may be put into the hands of the pupil; but even now it should be closed until the teacher has assured herself that the pupils are familar with every number fact required for the proper reading of page 9. To do this, the teacher should read the page aloud, Teacher the pupils filling the blanks. If there is Reads—Pupils Listen, and some hesitation on the part of many pupils, Supply Omitthis work should be several times repeated ted Numbers. before the pupils' books are opened. The number facts on the page having been mastered and reviewed, the pupil may with profit review them again *by reading the page*. This he should be able to do with little hesitation. If he has been properly prepared for the work, he should read the page in from two to three

*Hall's Elementary Arithmetic, page 9.

minutes.   Thus the work of the teacher is mainly aiding the pupil to prepare himself to read the page.

The order of procedure suggested in the foregoing paragraph may be applied to most of the pages of Book I. and to many pages of Book II.   This method will meet the approval of those who will take the trouble to test it, as well as of those who examine it from a psychological point of view.

Eye or Ear?

The third-grade pupil has already acquired a good degree of skill in getting thought from language addressed to the ear.   He has had a comparatively small amount of experience in getting thought from language addressed to the eye.   When he entered school for the first time, he had *listened* to language for about six years.   During the two years he has been in school he has *heard* a hundred times as many Pupils "Ear- thought symbols as he has *seen*.   For this Minded," reason he has vastly more skill in bringing so Far as Language is into consciousness that for which spoken Concerned. symbols stand than he has that which is expressed in written or printed symbols.   If the main task, then, is to image and to see relation, the problem can best be presented by addressing the ear. When the pupil opens the book, the same problems are re-presented by means of printed characters. While the work was being done orally, the task of the child was, (1) hearing symbols, (2) imaging, and (3) seeing relation.   When he takes the book, his task is, to him the more difficult one: (1) seeing symbols, (2) imaging, and (3) seeing relation. How long it will be necessary that he shall be thus assisted by the voice of the teacher depends upon the skill of the teacher and the ability of the pupil. The amount of oral preparatory work may be, from time to time, somewhat diminished; but it must not be omitted until the pupil has acquired the power easily to see in the printed symbol that for which it stands.

This method of procedure is a part of essential gradation in all the branches of study in the early years. The most successful teachers of reading are those who observe this psychological principle; who "tell the story," or at least a part of it—enough to arouse the interest of the pupil, and to put into operation his imaging activity—before the reading is attempted.

The "Spiral Advancement" Plan.

Says Le Fevre: "There are seven distinct numerical operations. * * * These seven operations are, by name, addition and its inverse, subtraction; multiplication and its inverse, division; involution and its two inverses, evolution and finding the logarithm."*

With the last three of these operations the pupil in the lower grades is not concerned. Expanding the fourth (division) into two thought processes, we have, as the distinct operations of arithmetic for the elementary school, (1) addition, (2) subtraction, (3) multiplication, (4) division (finding how many times one num-

*Number and Its Algebra, page 42.—D. C. Heath & Co.

ber is contained in another), and (5) division (finding a certain part of a number).

These five operations, the repetitions of which **The Elementary Spiral.** with a variety of magnitudes constitute the elementary spiral of the Werner Arithmetics, appear in regular order, five times on page 9, twice on page 10, five times on page 11, twice on page 96, and more than one hundred and fifty times in Book I. Each time a turn of the spiral appears something new is presented, differing only slightly from that with which the child is already familiar.

Small Numbers. At first the numbers are small and the problems easy. Very gradually greater numbers are introduced. (Compare the numbers on page 9 with those on any subsequent page—e. g., pages 11, 27, 41, 51, 61.) In some parts of the elementary **"Abstract Numbers."** spiral the so-called abstract numbers are employed; others are made up of five or more simple problems in applied arithmetic. (Compare the fifth set of problems on page 9 or 11 with **"Concrete Numbers."** the four preceding sets on the same page.) Gradually denominate numbers in considerable variety appear—e. g., numbers of inches and **Denominate Numbers.** feet on pages 10 and 12; numbers of pints, quarts, and gallons on pages 16 and 47. At first integral numbers are employed, but common **Integral Numbers.** fractions are early introduced.. See pages 45, 55, 65, 75, etc. Decimals appear on **Fractions.** pages 70, 80, 90, and as a turn of the spiral **Decimals.** on pages 155, 157, 195, 197.*

*Hall's Elementary Arithmetic, pages 153, 155; 193, 195.

Work Outside the Elementary Spiral.

The work which is outside the formal turns of the elementary spiral in Book I. may be considered under several heads, as follows:

1. The introduction of new magnitudes and such reductions (changes in form of expression) as are necessary that these may be employed in New Magnitudes and the spiral—may be added, subtracted, mul- tudes and tiplied, etc. See problems 1 to 4 on pages Reductions. 45, 55, 75, and 85; and pages 47 and 57.

2. Problems for practice similar to those in the spiral, but designedly presented out of the regular order. Sometimes a single problem involves Not in Reg- two or more of the fundamental operations, ular Order. as $\frac{2}{3}$ of 15 inches are — inches; 15 inches are $\frac{2}{3}$ of how many inches? See page 52, problems 15, 16, 17; page 62, problems 14 to 17. Sometimes the problems require both a reduction and one or more of the fundamental operations. See page 47, problems 14 to 20.*

3. The introduction of new number facts at regular intervals. See pages 41, 51, 61, 71, New Num- 81, etc. ber Facts.

4. Exercises to test and cultivate the imaging power, and at the same time to lead the pupil to see magnitude and magnitude relation in figures. Cultivate Im- See page 39;† pages 49, 59, 69, problems aging Power. 4 to 6; page 79. Moreover, the sequence of problems is such as will induce imaging. See page 41, prob-

*Problems 10 and 11 in Hall's Elementary Arithmetic.
† Hall's Elementary Arithmetic. pages 33 and 34.

lems 10, 11, 12, etc.; page 48, problems 1 to 8; page 51, problems 12, 13, 14, etc.; page 58, problems 1 to 12.

5. The introduction of new terms, with which the pupil is expected to become familiar by use rather **New Terms.** than by definition. See pages 53, 63, and 73.

6. Carefully graded exercises in figure manipula- **Ciphering.** tion. See last part of pages 44, 48, 50, 54, 58, 60, 64, 68, 70, etc.*

Further Explanation of the Plan of Book I.

It will be apparent that Book I. is not simply a collection of graded miscellaneous problems, but that *it is a book built on a plan.* The elementary spiral is at once the foundation upon which, and the **The Central** central column around which, are arranged **Column.** in somewhat regular order such exercises as will train the pupil in the discernment of quantity relation, and prepare him for the gradual ascent of the spiral. At every turn the fact is impressed upon him that the work involves only five numerical operations. (These he may at length learn to reduce to four.) He adds, subtracts, multiplies, divides, and divides. New magnitudes appear, but no new process appears, unless it be that of changing the form of quantitative expression—reduction. He soon discovers that he needs only to become familiar with a new kind of magnitude and the symbols that express it, learn to change the form of these expressions of quantity with-

*See last part of each page of Hall's Elementary Arithmetic.

out changing their value, and he can immediately make use of them in the spiral, and move forward and upward another turn.

It will be observed that the author has followed closely the recommendation of the Conference on Mathematics appointed by the Committee of Ten in providing "a greater number of exercises in simple calculation and in the solution of concrete problems" than have usually appeared in text-books for the third and fourth grades. *A Great Number of Simple Exercises.* While many concrete problems are given, the pupil is not allowed to lose sight of *the possible concreteness of all the problems given.* When he tells the meaning of an abstract problem (see *Telling the Meaning.* pages 157 and 197),* he thinks magnitude into the problem. When he tells the number story suggested by the problem (see pages 157 and 197), he thinks a particular kind of magnitude into *Telling the Number Story.* the problem. He is not permitted to forget that figures stand for magnitude and magnitude relation. The moment he is in danger of such forgetfulness he is asked to *tell the meaning—tell the number story.*

"Mental" or "Written"?

While a large part of the work is of the so-called *mental* order, there are hundreds of problems for the slate. These are carefully graded, and the pupil is expected to solve many of them "mentally" before he solves them with the aid of a pencil. See note at bottom of each of the following pages: 27, 28, 31,

*In Hall's Elementary Arithmetic, see pages 155 and 195.

32, 33, 34, 35.* The pupil who is thus taught will properly regard the pencil as a convenience in the doing of that which it is quite possible for him to do without using such an implement—even without figures.   He is led to think number as magnitude and number as relation often enough to prevent his falling into the habit of figure juggling.

In many instances a problem for the slate is preceded by a similar "mental" problem.   This plan not A "Mental" only leads the pupil to the solution of the Problem Followed by a more difficult problem, but it insures his lowed by a Problem for grasp of the number relations before he the Slate. begins the figure process.   This feature of the Werner Arithmetics is believed to be new and valuable.   See pages 172, 173, 212, 227, 240, 247, 248, 249.†

Multiplying by a Fraction.

Great emphasis is put upon the importance of leading the pupil to observe the meaning of problems in multiplication, particularly when the multiplier is a fraction or a mixed number.   See page 114; page 126, foot-note; page 129, problem 4, foot-note; page 136, foot-note; page 146, problem 4; pages 165 and 166; page 175, problems 14 and 15; page 176, problem (c); page 185, problems 14 and 15; pages 206, 207, and 208.‡

*In Hall's Elementary Arithmetic, see Suggestions to Teachers, pages 242, 243. Note especially the suggestions with reference to the work on pages 11, 12, 13, 14, and 15.
†In Hall's Elementary Arithmetic, see pages 165, 166, 167, 168.
‡In Hall's Elementary Arithmetic, page 104, and first three notes page 246.

The Double Aspect of Division.

The two thought processes in division are made prominent throughout the book. The author does not think it practicable to lead the child to see magnitude and magnitude relation in the figure Two Thought manipulation of division without making Processes. this distinction.   The psychologist may be right who regards all division (in the sense in which the term is employed in arithmetic) as the process of finding how many times one number is contained in another; who declares that we find one fifth of a number by finding how many times five is contained in the number. But the author of the Werner Arithmetics is unwilling to concede that the figure process of division can be well taught without presenting the subject to the pupil in its double aspect.   True, when required to "divide $2465 by 5," he may be led to divide 2465 by 5, or $2465 by $5, and then to interpret the result.   But this does not seem to be the direct and pedagogical method of approaching the subject.   It is immeasurably better that the pupil should see, before he performs the figure process, that if he is required to "divide $2465 by 5," he must find one fifth $2465 ÷ 5. of $2465; and if he is required to "divide $2465 ÷ $5. $2465 by $5," he must find how many times $5 is (or are) contained in $2465.   This method puts the seeing of magnitude relation into the foreground, and relegates figure manipulation to the rear, to be brought forward whenever it is needed as a convenience in seeing relation.   The importance which the

author attaches to the making of this distinction in
the division problems may be seen by examining the
following in Book I.:   *Page 15; last half of page 21;
page 26, problems at bottom of page, and foot-note;
pages 36 and 37; page 58, problems near the bottom
of page, and foot-note; page 60, last line of problems,
and foot-note; page 64, problems 4 and 5; page 70,
last line of problems, and foot-note; page 74, problems 3 and 4; page 78, problems near bottom of page,
and foot-note; page 80, last line of problems, and foot-
note; page 83, problems 12 to 19, and foot-notes,
etc.   It will be observed that this distinction is also
made in the last two processes in each turn of the
elementary spiral.

Division of Fractions.

The foregoing method is essential as a preparation
for the study of division of common and decimal fractions.   If the young pupil is expected to deal with
fractional units, these must be approached on the
magnitude side, otherwise figure juggling will be the
inevitable result of the effort.   Before attempting to
divide a fraction by a fraction, a fraction by an
integer, or an integer by a fraction, he must have
a clear conception of what he wishes to do—what he
is to find.   A pupil may be taught to *"Invert the
divisor and proceed as in multiplication,"* and be utterly
ignorant of the relation of the quantities involved.
He can get the answer; and when a few years later he

*In Hall's Elementary Arithmetic, see page 15; page 21, problems 11 to 14;
page 30; page 64, problems 1, 2, 3, 4; page 74, problems 1, 2, 3, 4; page 84, problems 1, 2; page 94, problems 1, 2. See also problems at bottom of pages 64 and 65,
74 and 75, 84 and 85, etc.

is required to "explain division of fractions," he can commit to memory the "explanation" provided by the teacher. Perhaps it never occurs to the teacher that the "explanation" is an attempt to put quantity and quantity relation into symbols from which these should never have been allowed to escape. The pupil who is well taught will not for any great length of time use symbols that are devoid of content. True, when quite familiar with a set of symbols he may very properly use them without stopping at every turn to bring into consciousness their real content; but he *should be able* to do this whenever danger of obscurity makes it necessary. He should *always be able* to see through the symbol that for which it stands. Inability on the part of the pupil to "concrete" a figure problem—to tell its meaning before solving it, and to tell a suggested number story after solving it—is a certain indication that symbol manipulation is coming too rapidly and too prominently into the foreground of the child's thoughts.

There are three kinds of problems in division of fractions that need especial attention with respect to their meaning. Examples of these follow:

I.

$$\$8 \div \$\tfrac{1}{2} = \qquad 8 \div \tfrac{1}{2} = \qquad \$\tfrac{1}{2} \div \$\tfrac{1}{4} = \qquad \tfrac{1}{2} \div \tfrac{1}{4} =$$

$$\$4 \div \$.5 = \qquad 4 \div .5 = \qquad \$\tfrac{1}{2} \div \$2 = \qquad \tfrac{1}{2} \div 2 =, \text{ etc.}$$

Any one of the above problems may be regarded as meaning, *Find how many times*, etc.; that is, each number is thought of as a magnitude, the problem being to find the ratio of the first to the second.

2.

$$\$\tfrac{1}{2}\div4= \qquad \tfrac{1}{2}\div4= \qquad \$8\tfrac{1}{2}\div4= \qquad 8\tfrac{1}{2}\div4=$$
$$\$.8\div4= \qquad .8\div4= \qquad \$2.4\div4= \qquad 2.4\div4=, \text{ etc.}$$

Any one of the above problems may be regarded as meaning, *Find one fourth of*, etc.; that is, the first number stands in consciousness for magnitude, the second for ratio. The problem is to find the other magnitude.

3.

$$\$6\div\tfrac{1}{2}= \qquad \$\tfrac{1}{2}\div\tfrac{1}{4}= \qquad \$15\div2\tfrac{1}{2}= \qquad \$275\div2.5=$$

Here the first number in each problem stands for magnitude and the second for ratio. The problem, as in No. 2, is *to find the other magnitude*. The fact that the ratio is a fraction or mixed number makes it somewhat more difficult of interpretation. The pupils of the lower grades should not be confronted with such problems as these. For the method of approach to the third variety of problems in division of fractions, see Book II., page 162.* No examples of this kind appear in the Werner Arithmetics on any page preceding the one mentioned above.

Werner Arithmetic, Book II.†

Here the main spiral along which the pupil advances is made up of the following topics: (1) Simple Numbers, (2) Common Fractions, (3) Decimals, (4) Denominate Numbers, (5) Measurements, (6) Ratio and

---

*The work here referred to is not given in the Hall Arithmetics in the form in which it is given in the Werner Arithmetic, Book II

†The first 149 pages of Hall's Complete Arithmetic are nearly identical with the first 149 pages of the Werner Arithmetic, Book II.

Proportion, (7) Percentage, (8) Review, and (9) Miscellaneous Problems. Two pages are devoted to percentage and one page to each of the A Topic is other topics. Thus each complete turn of Re-presented on Every this larger spiral occupies exactly ten pages Tenth Page. of the book. This plan is adopted as a convenience for reference and for review.

In passing over the book for the first time the pages should be assigned in their regular order, as in any other book. But a topic may be Pages to be reviewed by taking every tenth page; thus, Assigned in Regular if after passing over the first one hundred Order. pages of the book the class seems weak in the work in common fractions, review pages 12, 22, 32, 42, 52, etc. If decimals is the troublesome subject, Can be review pages 13, 23, 33, 43, 53, etc. If, Reviewed by Topic. for instance, page 127 seems too difficult for the pupil, review page 117, or pages 107 and 117, or pages 97, 107, and 117. This plan enables the teacher easily to select those parts of the book for review which are in the direct line of preparation for the special difficulty confronting the pupil.

The elementary spiral is not lost sight of in Book II. It appears, either in part or complete, on many of the common-fraction pages and upon The Elementary Spiral some of the decimal pages. See pages 72, tary Spiral in Book II. 82, 92, 102, and problems at the bottoms of pages 13, 23, 33, 43, 53, etc. On the first few common-fraction pages (12, 22, 32, 42) multiplication is omitted from the spiral. This is done for the purpose of throwing together and putting emphasis upon those processes in fractions in which it is necessary or convenient to operate with two or more fractions having like denominators.

Simple Numbers.

Under this head the pupil is gradually made familiar with the terms, *exact divisor, odd number, even number, integral number, fractional number, mixed number, prime number, composite number, factor, prime factor, multiple, common multiple, and least common multiple.* He is taught to multiply by any number of tens, any number of hundreds, etc.; to divide by any number of tens, hundreds, etc. He learns the meaning of the term *average,* and solves problems involving the use of simple numbers in great variety. See pages 11, 21, 31, 41, 51, 61, etc.

Common Fractions.

Under this head the pupil is taught to apply the elementary spiral to every variety of problems in common fractions. By a frequent requirement to "tell the meaning" and to "tell the suggested number story," the magnitude idea is kept prominent in the mind of the pupil while he learns to manipulate fraction symbols. "Three-story fractions" and "mathematical monstrosities" do not appear in the book. All the processes are taught with fractions having small denominators. Indeed, only such fractions as are needed in the solution of ordinary business problems are here introduced. See pages 12, 22, 32, 42, 52, 62, etc.

Decimals.

Here again the elementary spiral appears; but at first no fractions with denominators greater than 1000 are introduced. As in common fractions, the magnitude idea is made prominent. Here again the pupil is asked to "tell the meaning." By this plan the child knows how to "point off" his answer before he begins the figure process. He is not allowed to multiply, for instance, by .4 until he knows that this means, *find 4 tenths of the multiplicand.* To find 4 tenths, he must first find 1 tenth. He discerns before he begins the process of multiplication that he is simply to find 4 times 1 tenth of the multiplicand.

He is not allowed to divide $.385 by $.005 until he knows that he is to find how many times 5 thousandths are contained in 385 thousandths. Knowing this, his figuring is in no way different from that necessary to find how many times 5 bushels are contained in 385 bushels. He is not allowed to divide $.385 by 5 until he knows that he is to find 1 fifth of $.385. Knowing this, his figure work is in no respect different from that necessary to find 1 fifth of 385 bushels.

A problem having been solved, the pupil may be required to "tell the suggested number story"—that is, to give an example from real or prospective experience in which the given figure process may be employed. To make this possible, no unreal or impracticable problems are introduced.

Not a problem appears in Book II. that does not have its easily found parallel in the outside world,

usually very close to, if not a part of, the child's experience or observation.   See pages 13, 23, 33, 43, 53,
63, etc.

Denominate Numbers.

Instead of presenting the denominate number tables
to be committed to memory in two or three lessons,
the different units of measurement are gradually introduced into the problems given under this head.   Thus,
on page 14, we have problems involving dollars, tons,
an_ pounds; on page 24, bushels, tons, and pounds;
on page 54, feet, rods, and miles; on page 74, feet,
rods, yards, inches, miles, tons, pounds, dollars, and
cents.   Moreover, on these pages, and on the review
and miscellaneous pages (19 and 20, 29 and 30, 39
and 40, etc.), the units of measurement that were
treated in Book I. are kept constantly before the pupil.
The spiral advancement plan, giving opportunity as
it does for a most systematic, frequent, and thorough
review, enables the teacher to see that the *new* is
always related to the *old* in the mind of the pupil.
See pages 14, 24, 34, 44, 54, 64, etc.

Measurements.

All arithmetic has to do with measurement.   As
has been said, the number idea originates in measurement, and in the end the number processes are applied
to measurement.   But there are special phases of this
work which may properly be considered under this
head, the word *measurements* being here used in a
restricted sense.

Linear, surface, and solid measurements are the

subdivisions of this topic. The problems are especially adapted to the training and development of the imaging power. Indeed, length, area, and volume are the extension elements of all visual and motor images. Even weight, intensity, value, or temperature may be thought of (imaged) as length, area, or volume. Hence, by far the greater number of our images involve these extension elements. No work in mathematics can be more important than the training of the pupil to bring easily into consciousness images of these kinds of magnitude.

Here, as elsewhere, sequence has much to do with the training value of a set of problems. If each of twenty consecutive problems calls for the area of a square, and the figure process of each is quite long, there will be little imaging and much figure manipulation on the part of the pupil solving them. If problem 1 calls for area, problem 2 for perimeter, problem 3 for area, problem 4 for perimeter, etc.; or problem 1 deals with a square, problem 2 with a cube, problem 3 with a square, problem 4 with a cube, etc., and if the figure manipulation is easy, the emphasis will be upon imaging. This is as it should be; for, as has been said before, the difficult task is not in seeing magnitude relation, but in imaging the related magnitudes. See pages 15, 25, 35, 45, 55, 65, etc.

Ratio and Proportion.

Here the pupil is especially exercised in seeing number as magnitude and number as relation. Careful attention to the sequence of problems again puts the emphasis upon imaging and seeing relation. "*One fourth of 20 is —, 20 is ¼ of —*," is a better sequence for training in seeing relation than, "*One fourth of 20 is —, one fourth of 24 is —.*" Note the sequence of problems on pages 16, 26, 36, 46, 56, 66, etc.; also on pages 136 and 146.

Percentage.

It is believed that the subject of percentage as found on pages 17 and 18, 27 and 28, 37 and 38, 47 and 48, etc., is arranged in such a step-by-step order that no pupil who is properly prepared to undertake the work will find serious difficulty in its mastery. With very little assistance, the pupil should be able to take these steps. Page 17 is preparation for page 18; and pages 17 and 18 are preparation for pages 27 and 28. The lessons should be assigned in the regular order of the pages, as in any other book; but if the percentage problems on any page are found too difficult for the pupil, he need not necessarily be given assistance, but simply directed to review the percentage problems on the pages preceding that on which the difficulty appears. Indeed, this might properly be given as a very general direction. It is not best that the teacher should solve problems for the pupil, or show him how to solve them. If they are too heavy for him, *give him those which he can solve, and so lead up to and over the difficulty.*

Werner Arithmetic, Book III.*

No arithmetic built on the spiral advancement plan can be complete unless it at length leads the pupil to that point from which he may be able to survey the subject as a whole, and assists him in the doing of this. Hence, classification and generalization are the features of Book III. But here, as in Book II., in answer to a very general demand, the number of topics treated is by no means so great as the number found in the arithmetics of twenty years ago.

The fundamental operations in their application to simple numbers, decimals, United States money, denominate numbers, and literal quantities are treated briefly under the four general heads—addition, subtraction, multiplication, and division. The other topics presented are, properties of numbers, common fractions, percentage and its applications, ratio and proportion, powers and roots, and the metric system; to which are added a special chapter (page 231†) on denominate numbers, one on short methods, and many practical problems.

The spiral advancement plan is followed in the gradual introduction of elementary work in algebra and geometry. See pages 17, 18, 19; 27, 28, 29; 37, 38, 39; 47, 48, 49, etc.‡ The algebra work, especially, is closely correlated with the work in arithmetic. Six pages treating of figure notation are followed by two pages of algebraic notation; six pages treating of

* Or Complete Arithmetic, Part II.
† Complete Arithmetic, page 371.
‡ Complete Arithmetic, pages 157, 158, 159; 167, 168, 169; 177, 178, 179, etc.

addition as it appears in arithmetic are followed by two pages of algebraic addition, etc.   In many parts of the book, particularly· in fractions (see pages 87, 88, 97, 98*) and in proportion (see pages 197 and 198†), the literal notation is an invaluable aid in the generalization of the work in arithmetic.

Problems which "perplex and exhaust the pupil without affording any really valuable mental discipline" have been omitted.

The Werner Series of Arithmetics.

In the series as a whole, the author has attempted to "abridge and enrich" the subject of arithmetic. **The Abridgment.** The abridgment consists in omitting much that has heretofore been regarded as essential, particularly work involving long and difficult figure processes that have no parallel in ordinary business arithmetic, and but little if any disciplinary value. Such phases of commercial arithmetic as are unintelligible to the average child of twelve or fourteen years are also omitted.

The enrichment consists in the introduction of a large number of simple, concrete problems, all of **The Enrichment.** which have their parallel in the environment of the average pupil.

The entire series presents over fifteen thousand problems.   Those in Book I. are arranged into and around the elementary spiral—addition, subtraction, **Book I.** multiplication, division, and division.   Into this spiral at somewhat regular intervals appear easy

* Complete Arithmetic, pages 227, 228; 237, 238.
† Complete Arithmetic, pages 337, 338.

problems with integral numbers, common fractions, decimals, United States money, and denominate numbers.

The problems in Book II. are arranged into the larger spiral made up of seven topics; namely, simple **Book II.** numbers, common fractions, decimals, denominate numbers, measurements, ratio and proportion, and percentage. Each turn of the spiral covers ten pages of the book.

The problems in Book III. lead the pupil into a survey of the subject as a whole, with its usual divisions and subdivisions, all of which are sup- **Book III.** plemented by elementary exercises in algebra and geometry.

The Hall Arithmetics.

The Elementary Arithmetic is substantially the same as the Werner Arithmetic, Book I.

The Complete Arithmetic is made up of Werner Books II. and III. somewhat abridged.

The Hall Arithmetics are made on the same general plan as the Werner Arithmetics. They are designed for those who desire a somewhat briefer course than that provided by the three-book series.

The author and publishers cannot be otherwise than delighted with the reception that has already been accorded in the East and in the West to "The New Arithmetics." They were wrought out in the schoolroom, because the writer felt the need of them

in his own work.   They are the outgrowth of more
than a third of a century's experience in presenting
this subject to pupils and to teachers.   If now they
shall prove in a large degree helpful to the thousands
of teachers and tens of thousands of pupils into whose
hands they have already found their way, it will be
a source of immeasurable satisfaction to their author.

It is difficult to complete this little monograph
without the introduction of the personal pronoun of
the first person.   In thanking one's personal friends,
good form does not demand the pretended conceal-
ment of one's own personality behind *the author*, or
by the use, even, of the editorial *we*.

I beg to thank most sincerely the hundreds (I might
almost say thousands) of friends, many of whose faces
I have never seen, who have taken the trouble to
express in no doubtful terms their appreciation of the
results of my endeavor to "abridge and enrich" the
work in arithmetic for the common schools.

I desire especially to express my gratitude to my
good friend Orville T. Bright, of Chicago, to whom
I am indebted, more than to any other teacher or
superintendent, for early recognition of the value of
my work, and for timely assistance in bringing it to the
attention of an enterprising publishing house, whose
services have already made me, in a sense, the teacher
of MORE THAN A QUARTER-MILLION PUPILS.

F. H. H.

JACKSONVILLE, ILLINOIS, May, 1900.

The Longest Possible Test

DeKalb, Illinois, June, 1900.

In the summer of 1896, while superintendent of the schools of Austin, Illinois, I received a copy of the Werner Arithmetic, Book I. This book had at that time been before the public less than one month. I had during the previous year observed the work of the author in the Waukegan schools, and was in sympathy with it. I expected a book aggressively devoted to meeting the essential needs of the grades for which it was intended, and meeting them fully; a book adapted by its clear discernment of what matter to present, of the order and rate of its presentation, by its stead-fast adherence to the main line of its purpose, by the ingenuity and simplicity of its method and arrangement, and by its sharp self-limitation of range—adapted thus unfailingly to reach its end.

I was not dissapointed. The book went beyond my measure for it. The unity was very marked; the holding of the several lines of thought, in clear, close relationship, unslackened. I was convinced that it was almost, if not quite, the ideal book for its place in the curriculum.

In the autumn of 1896, we gave Book I a trial in our schools. At an early date it was adopted for use in all the grades for which it was designed. When the other books of the series appeared (Book II in 1897, and Book III in 1898), these, too, were adopted. I have thus had continuous experience with the Werner Arithmetics as long as it is possible for any one to have had such experience.

From my own observation, and from the unanimous sentiment of my teachers, I am led to reaffirm the opinions early formed and expressed. Intelligent fidelity to the author's plan results in stronger grasp, clearer insight, greater facility, and more zest in dealing with numbers. The teacher is helped even more than the pupil.

(*Signed*) NEWELL D. GILBERT,
Supt. DeKalb Public Schools.

Formerly Supt. Austin Public Schools.

Dearborn School
Boston, Mass.

BOSTON, MASS., January 26, 1900.
WERNER SCHOOL BOOK COMPANY.

Dear Sirs:—The Werner Arithmetics by Frank H. Hall meet my hearty approval because of their simplicity and wise classification. They embody Prof. Hall's belief that number has two aspects, magnitude and ratio. These books also make a close connection between mental arithmetic and written arithmetic; they require the pupil to do his own thinking and make his own rules. The problems grow more and more difficult, but they change gradually.

These books call for "the story," in which the child, *and not the teacher*, makes up a variety of examples; reviews are regularly introduced, and drill is never lost sight of. In short, these books seem to be made by one who understands a child's mind, and is anxious to do what is best for the development of that mind.

My teachers are highly pleased with the books.

Yours truly,

C. F. KING.

The Public Schools
City of Beatrice
Beatrice, Nebraska

BEATRICE, NEB., March 31, 1900.

WERNER SCHOOL BOOK COMPANY,
Chicago, Illinois.

Dear Sirs:—We adopted the Werner Arithmetics in our schools last August, and have been watching the results very closely. They were chosen from all other arithmetics because we regarded them as the best published, and they have fully come up to our expectations.

In the first place, arithmetic is no longer the meaningless mass of abstract computations that have in the past been the bugbear of both pupils and teacher. The Werner Arithmetics make both study and teaching a delight.

In the second place, the pupils have their mathematical powers developed, and at the same time learn to apply these powers along practical lines, and acquire a knowledge of numbers that will always be of use to them. The books are also valuable for the omission of many unnecessary subjects that have cumbered our text-books in the past.

You are to be congratulated upon the publication of these excellent books. Progressive teachers will welcome them wherever they can be introduced.

Very truly yours,
J. W. DINSMORE,
Superintendent of Schools.

NEW HAVEN, CONN.

WERNER SCHOOL BOOK COMPANY:

After the examination of various text-books, the supervisory staff, by a vote of eight out of the ten, recommended the Werner Arithmetic, Book III, and it was unanimously adopted by the Board of Education. Among the reasons given for their choice were these:

"The book omits superfluous subjects in Arithmetic."

"The exercises are more nearly like the combinations of business than other books, therefore the tone of the book is practical, and it is believed it will appeal strongly to pupils."

"The Algebra and Geometry exercises SUPPLEMENT the Arithmetic exercises, and are not simply additions to the text."

"The book not only compels thought, but induces it."

"Mensuration is carried through the book in a most admirable way."

"The admirable page arrangement of the book makes it simple and plain for teachers to use."

"The arrangement of the book is ideal."

Personally, I believe the Werner book the most rational contribution that has been made to arithmetical text-books for the higher grammar grades.

Yours sincerely,

C. N. KENDALL,

Superintendent of Schools.

The DeGarmo Language ====== Series ======

A COURSE IN ENGLISH FROM PRIMARY GRADES TO HIGH SCHOOL

LANGUAGE LESSONS

By CHARLES DE GARMO, Ph. D.

Professor of the Science and Art of Education, Cornell University, Ithaca, N. Y.

ELEMENTS OF ENGLISH GRAMMAR

By GEORGE P. BROWN
Former Superintendent of Schools, Indianapolis, Ind.

Assisted by CHARLES DE GARMO

PRICE LIST

Language Lessons, Book One, 145 pages - - - 30 cents
Language Lessons, Book Two, 188 pages - - - 40 cents
Beautifully and Copiously Illustrated.
Complete Language Lessons, in one volume, 256
pages, over 200 illustrations - - - - - - 50 cents
Elements of English Grammar, 256 pages - - 60 cents

SEND FOR DESCRIPTIVE CIRCULARS OF OUR UP-TO-DATE

Epoch-Making Text-Books

Samples to Teachers for examination at special rates.
Liberal terms for introduction and exchange.

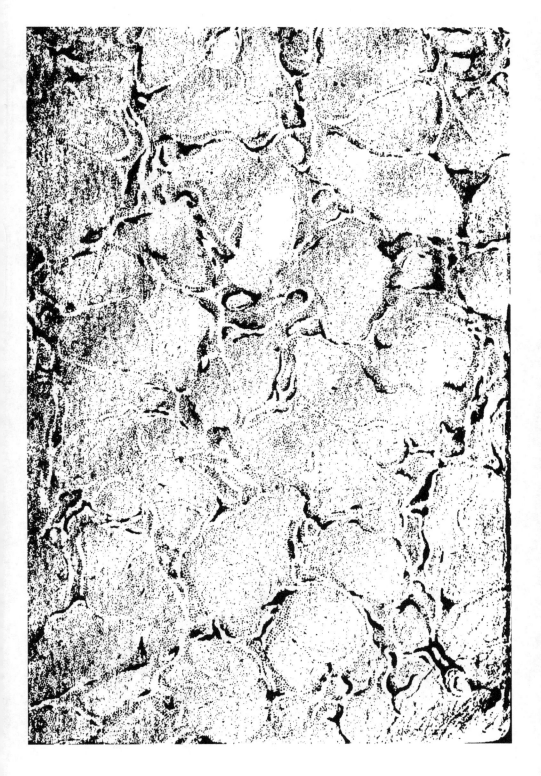

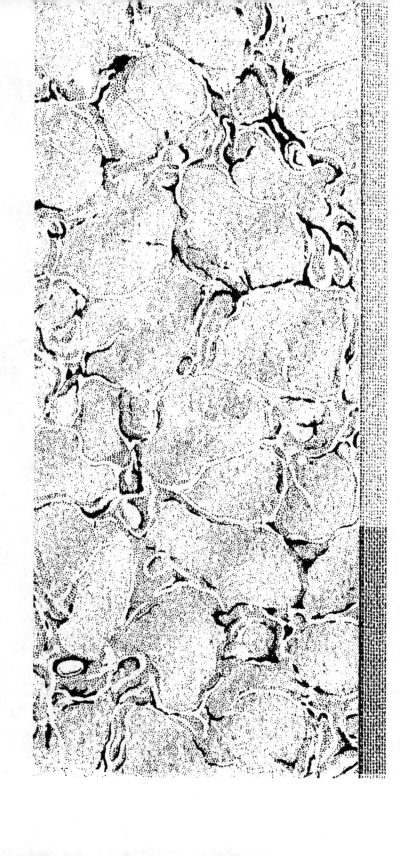